Prayers to pray without really trying

Prayers to pray without really trying

By Jeanette Struchen

J. B. LIPPINCOTT COMPANY
PHILADELPHIA AND NEW YORK

To Debbie

To the reader

Some people collect stamps as a hobby. I write prayers. Ideas come from rubbing shoulders with daily life. Listening for words and looking for ideas keeps me aware of God in the ordinary.

God is not a celestial genie and in prayer I need not pretend to be that which I am not, believe that which I cannot, or stack up high-sounding phrases which do not sound like me. God knows me best as a simple human being touched by an eagerness to be useful and a joy to be contagious.

It is my hope that you will find these prayers as invigorating as fresh air and as practical as an umbrella in rain.

Prayers to pray without really trying

Remember that pesky problem I told you about last
  night, Lord?
It looked like a real blockbuster but a ray of
  morning light punched holes in it and the whole
  thing went up in smoke.

Thank you for this new loose freedom!
Thank you for this new sense of fresh air!
Thank you for this brand new morning!
Thank you for this personal miracle!

I feel so lighthearted maybe I'll stuff the
  whole day with happy nonsense and juggle the
  hours in joy and adoration.

Amen

O Lord what happens to my threads of conviction?

Today demands a strong unbendable will;
    I am brittle.
Today demands energy, whole and vital;
    I am weak.
Today demands risks, uninsured and incalculable;
    I am afraid.

Help me keep a strong hand to the plow and without
    looking back expose ideas which suck life out of
    my courage and eat new shoots of my good intentions.

I want to be a strong dependable follower.

Amen

O God give me courage to keep facing the world.

I don't want to turn my back.

This is not an age to turn a deaf ear or make judgments
through tranquilizers.
Widen the framework of my mind that in it I shall find
growing identity.
Keep me from being nearsighted and plagued with blind
spots.
The world is full of great machinery which creates good
so keep me from getting involved with
little gadgets.
Show me where to bury the mask for my daily act and
how to avoid props which screen me from reality.

Amen

Lord why does she call me on the phone?

She jumps from one subject to another like
   they were hot from Associated Press.
I couldn't care less about the new arrangement
   of her gall bladder or what happened to the
   lawn mower.
Yesterday I must have been kidding when I prayed
   to be a better listener.

Aren't there any ground rules?

Amen

Lord I need patches on my faith.
The cloth of courage has worn thin.
The threads of joy have been cut.
The pattern of right and wrong has faded out.
I don't pray for more love but for strength
   to move the love I already have.
I don't pray for a new conscience but for sense
   enough to scrape barnacles off the old one.
I don't pray to be commander in chief over my life
   but a trustworthy private on a worthwhile mission.
I don't pray for a medal but for loyalty in my heart.

Amen

[14]

Today I feel like a feather, Lord.

Fresh air is blowing through my stuffiness
    and leaves me with a whiff of delight.

I stand on tiptoe watching the debut of another Spring.

Amen

O God today
I do not ask to be a mighty leader
   but a loving, faithful follower.
I do not ask to be charged with vibrant enthusiasm
   but nourished with quiet refreshment.
I do not ask to be filled to the brim every minute
   but now at day's end let me be thankful.
I do not ask for enough power that my lamp of faith
   will never flicker
   but devotion that I shall not leave unguarded the truth
   that has been entrusted to me.
In quietness help me feel new joy.
In patience help me translate ideas into useful vessels.
In surrender help me follow the plain path of service.
In gentleness help me be a loving servant.
Use me as your child—eager for a pure heart and steady faith
   to tell of the love that will not let me go.

                               Amen

Lord thank you for apprentice people
  who don't pretend answers before asking questions.
Thank you for enthusiastic people
  who capture ideas and run with them.
Thank you for fun people
  who carry life lightly with flags of joy.
Thank you for generous people
  who adopt unadoptables and live for others.
Thank you for unassuming people
  who don't stack their assets for display.
Thank you for deep people
  who rub against us with perspective and vision.
Are these the meek inheritors of the earth?

Amen

Seems like yesterday that he was handed to me
  in a blue blanket. Where have the years gone, Lord?
I remember the way he cried while splashing buckets of
  water over a goldfish as it lay helpless on the kitchen floor
  and the day he carried home a tadpole and sat down
  to watch it turn into a frog.
I remember the rumpus he raised when the girl next door
  moved and then suddenly he started practicing "America"
  in the bathtub when a marine moved in.
Then there were the laughs we had when he mowed the
  zigzag line down the yard and promised to buy me
  all the bubble gum in the world when he grew up.
And it was exciting to watch his cycle of interests
  switch from Tinkertoys to intellectual activities.

Now here he is, Lord, so big and strong, and ready
  for the first grade.

Amen

Am I supposed to be searching for something, God?

Today I am full of joy chasing the good life.
Tomorrow the joy may drop out of me and I'll be
    chasing vague promises.
Today I've stuck my neck out for other people
    but
Tomorrow I may stand on the corner unconcerned about
    anybody but myself.
In daylight I can't feel any inner flame at all.
I think it's easier to be holy in the dark.
If all this is trying to teach me something,
Remember, Lord, I learn slowly.

Amen

Help the offbeat,
Capture their rebellion,
Listen to their song of forsakenness,
Reach them in their exile.
But let some of their courage rub
   off on me, Lord.

I don't want to be swallowed by the
   whale of conformity.

Amen

Lord, let me gather standing room in your presence this
  morning.
I do not ask to be shining and radiant. I do not pray for
  visions
but for a fresh consciousness at the center of my being.

As your child keep me turned toward you all day. I shall lean
often because I know how little I know, how uneven my
  tempo, how
shifty my intentions, how blind even in light, how un-
  raveled even
with my well-woven design.

To stand in your presence this morning is to stand on holy
  ground.
Lord, take all my building material—spirit, mind, will—
  and use
each one today.

May the words from my mouth, the intentions from my
  heart, and the
joy from my spirit build something significant and un-
  shakable.

Amen

I saw a box of false eyelashes today, Lord,
And a bottle of hair color;
I saw a package of heel inserts to make me taller
And fingernails to make mine more glamorous.

Lord, I'd like to be beautiful but
   don't let me be artificial.

Amen

The pressure is on, Lord.

I have the feeling I'm battling a deadline
to DO something in order to BE somebody—
   or is it vice versa?

Do you have a shelter from the future?

Amen

"Won't you have one?" said my date
   as drinks came my way.

Suddenly, Lord, I knew the face of unacceptance.

Help me understand when I am not understood
   and
Keep me aware of your presence in all my
   daily choices.

Amen

O God

Don't let me believe so much that I stop asking questions
Or question so much that I stop believing.
Don't let me spread myself so thin that I slip out
 of responsibility
Or get so burdened with responsibility that I forget
 to refuel myself.
Don't let me get so involved asking "What is man?" that I
 forget to ask "Who am I?"
Or gorge myself on "Who am I?" and pick lightly at the
 destiny of man.
Don't let me try so hard to be somebody to others
That I forget to be somebody to you.
Don't let me stand so long on the corner of frivolity
That I ignore the road to real joy.
Don't let my love get sticky sweet so that it loses its capacity
 to be rigorous
Or become so rigorous that the sweetness melts and runs
 away.

Just keep me in balance.

Amen

Lord help me take advice.
Help me make room for correction,
Help me see light in criticism,
Help me feel reason through my emotion,
Help me connect even in conflict.

Amen

I don't want to be a leader, Lord.
Everyone seems to be marching to a different drum
   and my legs ache in the parade.
I get sick of hearing about involvement and
   responsible leadership.

I guess I had better be a follower.

Could you use a plain and ordinary follower?

Amen

What were you celebrating last night, God?

You pulled out all the stops!

Thank you for cracking thunder
   and for sweeping rain across roofs,
   for smacking it against windows,
   for shoving rocks into heaps,
   for floating branches like gum wrappers.
Thank you for letting me catch a squint of the
   whole celebration when you threw that flashing
   spotlight on it.
This morning the tulip is just as red
   and every slinky blade woke up with a clean face.
The birds are uproarious.
Every living thing whispers, "Thank you."

I must shine my shoes to walk the earth today.

                         Amen

Lord why can't my folks take me as I am
   rather than pushing me at what they
     expect me to be?

Was I shortchanged on patience?
Or are they long shots on hope?
When I break a little rule they make
   a federal case,

When I follow the rule they take it for granted.

Whoever wrote "Honor thy father and mother" should
  have had a footnote, "Give the kids a break."

Amen

How do you file your secrets, God—
By age or size?
By your purpose or by man's inquisitiveness?
Do you have an empty drawer where we could file
   obsolete feuds and moth-eaten resentments?
I hate to be after a bargain, Lord, but it would
   help to have a peace pill.
As it is one angry sneeze creates a world-wide
   headache.

Is peace filed mistakenly in a folder for
   man-do-it-yourself?

If so, we're about as progressive as a boomerang.
Or, on second thought, Lord, is extinction for
   more than dinosaurs?

Amen

O Lord, Christmas is not for children.

It's for the crying to give them hope.
It's for the joyous to make them thankful.
It's for the thoughtful to give them meaning.
It's for the lost to give them direction.
It's for the nearsighted to give them perspective.
It's for the poor to give them treasure.
It's for me to give you room.

Amen

There is a giant of joy inside me, Lord—
It gives me strength to stand on my convictions
    and whistle above my prejudices;
It makes me want to grow and give and love and sing.
    I doubt that I could sing very well,
        or give very much,
        or grow very tall,
So call me to usefulness quick before my giant
    gets tied down with strings of triviality.

Amen

O Lord deliver us from techniques to improve the world
    and
  fill us with great doses of patience.
Understanding takes time.
Concern takes time.
Love takes time.
Slow us down so we may explain the game—
Not everyone is getting to play.
Forgive us for hiding secret goals and sending in
    substitutes for ourselves.
Some have only a sketch of the playing field
    while others write the rules and pay for equipment—
    then limit participation.
We know the game is not part-time activity, our Father,
    but a surge for human survival. Involvement is
    our sacred obligation.

Amen

Thank you God for the good eyes you gave me.
First, I saw that lady pushing a stroller
and then the gray cat ran in front of us.
I could have sworn the telephone pole was stretched
right across the road and those kids on skate boards
zoomed in and out like flies at a picnic.
It was a harrowing ride around the park, Lord,
and I do see so much more from the back seat.

Amen

O God

Why is your love for me measureless
When I return it by the spoonful?
Why is your care for me infinite
When I accept it in fits and starts?
When your care is over everyone
Why do I sort out my friends by color?
When your spark has been hidden inside me
Why do I run in fevered pitch
    making the spark flicker?
When you know me in and out
Why do I keep adjusting my mask and pretending?
When you fill my heart with song and direction
Why do I chirp and fly in circles?
When you have made the world exciting and vast
Why do I keep on living in a capsule?

Amen

O God I am a better-late-than-never prodigal—
  Caught for inattention
    and
  On trial for squandering my Divine inheritance.
  Handcuff my ego but free my spirit.
  Condemn my laziness but acquit my intentions.
  Penalize my fake humility but accept my
    desire to improve.
  Judge my disobedience but pardon my delay in
    repentance.
Lord, above all, don't kill a fatted calf but just
  come to meet me.

Amen

Thank you, God, for the touch of holiness upon the earth this morning. Beyond the shepherds who ran and angels who hovered over a manger the idea dawns upon me that the word became flesh and lived among men.

Strike a new light in me that I may keep steady vigil
over dark places in my attitudes and actions.
Turn my little tune into great tidings of great joy—
I, too, am a listening shepherd.
Untwist the strain within me and draw it toward a quiet
manger where even oxen knew enough to kneel.
Fill my tarnished cup with wonder that I may reflect
something of your peace today.

On such a day I would not come with a paper-wrapped gift for all I am and all I have are yours. I have come with room in my heart for you—only for you.

Amen

Lord, we have a crisis here!
I called the emergency number in the yellow pages
 and finally ran to the neighbors for help.
The children are crying and my husband is stampeding
 the corral.
Dinner has already burned and the baby needs attention.

Do you suppose tomorrow is the day the TV repairman
 will come?

Amen

Life is proud and solitary, Lord, yet all men
    are strung in a common web.
  My deepest thoughts are silent thoughts.
  My most solemn moments are unshared.
  My loneliness is hidden in a mask of activity.
  My insecurity is carried in a secret pocket.
And over all, the great dark wings of death
    hover overhead and I am partly spent.

Love me, Lord, and all men, as we hover between birth
    into life and birth into eternity.

Amen

Lord I feel handicapped.
All week I have been out of joint at the office.
Yesterday my shell was cracked when the boss
  criticized my work
And today I got tongue-tied stammering an apology.
Honestly, I don't think the answer to personal
  security is a deodorant commercial,
  a stockbroker,
  or life insurance,

But when it gets down to basics do you suggest
  more grease in my elbow or more starch
  in my backbone?

                               Amen

I don't want to follow fads, Lord,
Yet I want to be popular.
I feel like I have a good personality but
I can't see the point of always being
  on the "in" crowd.
When drags are passed, keep me strong enough
  to resist temptation
  and wise enough not to brag about it.
Don't let me look stupid to the crowd or to myself
  for doing what is right.

Help me to be the best I know without apology.

Amen

O Lord shine me up on the inside.
Sometimes I get so dull that nothing reflects.
Turn me upside down and polish me anew.
I don't want to be a relic of the past
But alert in the reality of the present.

Amen

O God do you have a compass for me?
The days take off on jet wings and in such speed
   I lose perspective.
All the little things become too great and
   the great slip into insignificance.
Easily I lose my sense of direction and peck
   my way back halfheartedly.

My temperament goes up and down like an elevator.

   It is so hard to be stable in this crazy world.
I shift to and fro with every wind of doctrine.
   Just keep me from going in circles.

Amen

Am I expecting too much, Lord, if I want
   him to be a doctor or the President?
Everybody says he has great potential.
Maybe the pro teams will pick him.
   He has tremendous vitality
   and kicks like a veteran.

Perhaps he will be a comedian and make
   others as happy as he makes us.

Dreams are wonderful, Lord, and it's only
   6 more months until he'll be born.

Amen

I need a wrecking crew, Lord.
I keep building little shabby walls—
    ego to hide my shortcomings,
    pride to defend my dishonesty,
    personal desires to separate me from your will.
I put up foundations of prejudice and towers of
    overconfidence.
I pile up attitudes into blockades and fortify
    them with peashooter opinions.
I erect mighty convictions and stick them
    together with sand.

O God, let me take another squint at your blueprint
    for me.

Amen

Shave off the corners of my disposition, Lord.
I am a thorn in the flesh to others.
My temper is lashed to my unbendable will
    and
  knocks the breath out of my good intentions.
I stab others defending myself and that which
  passes as courage keeps me prisoner on a chain.

Lord, I'm shouting for help.

Amen

I don't have a map, Lord,
  yet consciously I know we are on the Jericho road.

We ignore the scream for help.
We push away tentacles of involvement.
We slip the shackles of responsibility.
We desert the masses for personal freedom.
We apply Band-Aids to heal deep wounds.
We offer advice instead of compassion.
We pick the world's sores and keep them infected.
We stare at our brother from the other side of the road.

Isn't there a Jericho bypass?

Amen

It was a wonderfully informative trip tonight, Lord.
I heard the last threatening shouts of parents to
   their offspring at bedtime
And saw the parting struggle of 2 teen-agers saying good
   night.
I felt the final rattle of windows as
   a neighborly stereo went off
And smelled someone's gentle pipe wafting from
   a secluded patio.
I caught the last spurts of a garden hose as
   indecisive fingers struggled for shutoff,
And tripped over a 2-wheeler left as a trap
   by some 9-year-old daredevil.
But the dog has been walked, Lord, and another day
   has come to pass.

Amen

O *God* give me a curious heart.

Today I heard giants of ideas—
   love is forever,
   faith made portable is witness,
   fear is a cockeyed but conquerable reality,
   convictions can waver but
   they shouldn't bob up and down.

Let me never throw away my searching self.
Keep me hounding the mysteries of life.
Keep me stretching for answers and blinking with wonder.
Keep me knocking at the door of knowledge searching
   after your will.

Amen

O *God* I nibble at the corners of self-discipline.
I want to take time to be holy but the clock strikes me
    into fevered pitch.
I want to grow but the ground is not always ready for
    planting.
I want to be your child but my many selves keep loyalty and
    love split into pieces.
I want to be a good citizen but it takes strength to
    hold up great attitudes.
O God, don't let me lean on excuses until the light fades
    within me. I would not want to go out on the road of life
    with a dim flashlight.

Amen

O God in the quietness this evening your love covers me
like a great tent.
I am aware that all day I have been going in and out
performing my little acts beneath its vastness.
As you have filtered light through the night sky filter it
through me.

> If I was forgetful today, prod me anew tomorrow.
> If I tried to jog along without help, forgive.
> If I sounded off key, retune me.
> If I prayed for peace but ran in fevered haste all day,
> try me again.
> If I forgot to stop at the well this morning, give me a
> new thirst.

Lord, stretch your quietness over all my awkward shapes.
Hold me at even pace all through this night. Quiet my
jagged edges and guide my many selves into one useful
self.

Amen

O God as you have made mountains and valleys in the earth so have you made them in me.

For moments when I stand on a peak and am filled with wonder, I am thankful.

For uplifted moments when I walk the quiet mountain path in light, I am thankful.

For moments when I feel you near and sense the print of joy upon me, I am thankful.

But every day is not a mountaintop and every moment is not filled with joy.

> When I walk in shadows, show me the way.
> When I trip on my bumpy inner self, uphold me.
> When I run and miss the beauty of the valley, forgive.
> When I stop trying for fear of falling, pace me.

During these days when I cannot run and tell or walk without being weary
help me stand by the well with my cup.

Amen

Thank you for my exciting, safe trip, Lord.

I picked cherry blossoms in Japan, dipped my toes
in the Mediterranean, and touched snow in Tibet.
I held my breath over an Alpine pass and heard cowbells
on the rocky slope.
I stood awe-struck in Westminster Abbey as immortal
greatness passed by and laughed as wee Highlanders
practiced their pipes.
I leaned to kiss the Blarney stone and waved at
royalty in Sweden.

Thank you, Lord, for man's glorious ability to create
joy from a travel folder.

Amen

O God Creator—who spills the firmament into my cup
And trails the stardust through the skies,
Who spreads the rainbow 'mid the rain
And beats the thunder 'gainst the earth,
Who shakes the clouds until they leak
And sprinkles dew down tiny blades,
Who splashes lightning o'er the hills
And squeezes sunbeams through the fog,
Who hides the buds in secret places
And beckons seasons to come forth,
Who strikes the hours of night and day
And counts the eggs within a nest,
Who plants the coral 'neath the sea
And strikes aflame some sleeping crater,
Who guides the seeds for human life
And leads the dying through the valley,
Who lifts the waves upon the seas
And spins the years into eternity—
Touch me again and make my life a miracle.

Amen

Lord is there an escape hatch from a forty-year wilderness?
    Loneliness is a trap in a desert.
    Stubborn inflexibility is digging ruts in sand.
    Imbedded grief is wearing thistles for a coat.
    Spiritual hunger is lack of an oasis.
    Chronic fear is an obstacle course to the
       promised land.
To get out of a wilderness, Lord, some people might
    pray for a compass but I need a burning bush.

Amen

O Lord take up the slack in me.
There is so much of me that loosely dangles
  without purpose.
Blow away the feathers in my head.
Get me off this binge of insensitivity.
Yank the blinders that keep me peeking at the world.
Never let me get so old that I can't feel growing pains
  or stay so young that somebody else
  shoulders my responsibility.
Shake the starch out of my mind and put it in my backbone.
Erase the wings from my tongue and hitch them to my
  actions.

Amen

Lord I've picked up a cinder in my eye.
It gives me blind spots
     and
Keeps me aware of my own discomfort.
Eyes are your gift to me;
Perspective is mine to you.
In such an age I don't want to be caught
     with lack of vision.

Amen

Lord I've been so busy adjusting a safety belt
   I forgot to watch the turn signals.

The hip generation has moved in and
   I am parading with a "do not disturb" sign.

Changing winds whip burning issues and
   I am caught with a drafty old philosophy.

Contagious rebels stab traditions and
   I'm quarantined with cold feet.

O God don't let my greatest action today
   be a push on a revolving door.

Amen

Lord get me out of this nest of antique collectors
   who keep dusting off trivia,
   polishing historic brass,
   and exhuming relics.

How about a passport into your vast universe
   and letting me stake out a galaxy or two?

   I want to be where the action is.

Amen

O God of life on both sides of the valley,
   thank you
  for this peek through the cloud of unknowing.

Never has eternity looked sweeter or more inviting.
Never any dearer since he passed the valley gate.
He wouldn't want fanfare, Lord, but give him
  room for quiet thinking.
Let him be happy with remembering and patient with
  waiting.

O Lord, eagerly I run to catch up and thank him again
  for his love.

Amen

O *God* this has been a long day's journey
   sealed in a tomb of fog.

I can't see a sign or marker and everything is
   Maltese gray, without shape.
I can't separate right from left before me
   or living from dead beside me.
I know fog can't be blasted or wished away
   but it rolls away when touched by
   rays of the sun.

Bless me, Father, with resurrection by sunlight.

                                        Amen

O God lift me out of my capsule existence.
Life is eternal. . . .
It comes with infinite meaning
    and
  vast dimension.
Save me from timidity like a teetering fledgling
  old enough for freedom
    but
  afraid to take wing.
Show me the dimension for living
    but
  keep me from flying in circles.
Call me with the old song
    but
  tune me to the new age.
Forgive me, Lord, if I chirp when I need
  to sing full-throated.

Amen

Create a Genesis in me, O God.
I want to be renewed and touched up.
When the spark of goodness flickers, fan it.
When the gift of life gets shabby edges, trim it.
Show me again that man crowns creation
    and
Reissue the orders to subdue the earth by love.

Amen

O *God* this morning
I bring my cup to be filled in the Divine Spring.
In this moment I hide from the confusion in the world
   to walk beside secret waterways and kneel
   to quench my thirst.
Take away the desert in my thinking that something fresh
   may grow for you.
Erase the mirage of my will and lead me to your oasis.

   Let water from the Divine Spring pour through
     and carry me beyond myself—
   Let it flow around the island of my selfishness.
   Let it flow over the rocks which trap and misdirect me.
   Let it wash away my daily pressure and buoy up joy
     within me.

Amen

O God make my heart a quiet place.
Help me remember that whether I stand on the peak
   or stumble in the valley I am in your care.
Support me that I shall not trip in this experience.
Steady my tremors with the knowledge that you have
   made me and will not drop me.
As you have given the bird a song and the butterfly
   wings give me an enduring trust.

Amen

Lord for such a day as this my lamp of faith has been lit.
Help me see my full responsibility to opportunity in this
   place.
Let me be eager to run the full course even though
   the finish line beckons me toward freedom and relaxation.
Hold me close, for you know I am more of a learner than a
      teacher, more of a follower than a leader.

I stand at the door and knock—

   For stillness within to make me a patient listener,
   For outpouring love to share in the fellowship,
   For freshness in my task to give worthy service,
   For patience without because of joy within.

Take the eager spirit which dwells in this tired body
   and use it hour by hour.

Amen